Activities We Do

We Help at Home

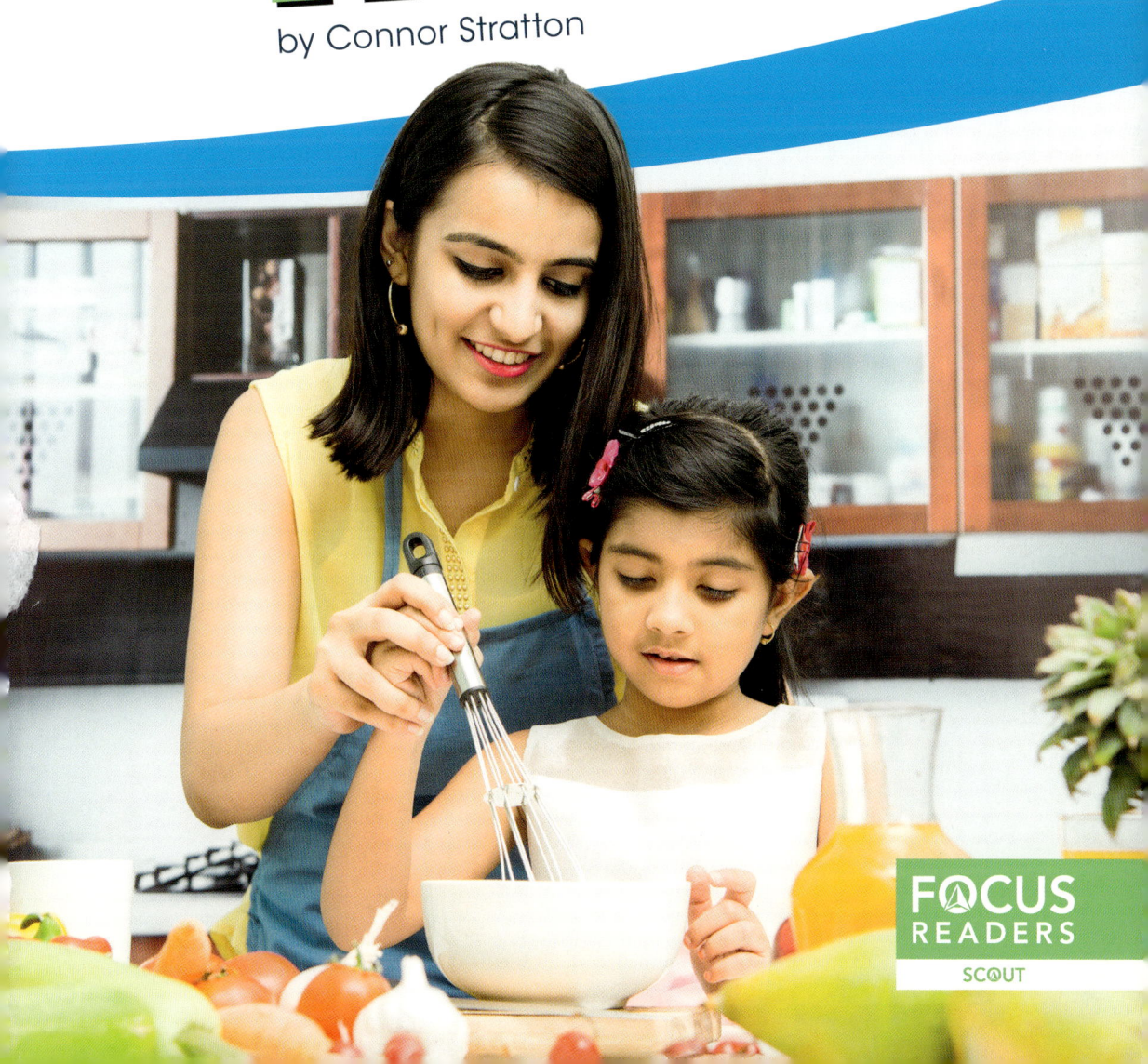

by Connor Stratton

www.focusreaders.com

Copyright © 2020 by Focus Readers, Lake Elmo, MN 55042. All rights reserved. No part of this book may be reproduced or utilized in any form or by any means without written permission from the publisher.

Focus Readers is distributed by North Star Editions:
sales@northstareditions.com | 888-417-0195

Produced for Focus Readers by Red Line Editorial.

Photographs ©: StockImageFactory.com/Shutterstock Images, cover, 1; Rawpixel.com/Shutterstock Images, 4, 7 (bottom), 13 (top); PeopleImages/iStockphoto, 7 (top), 15 (top); Yakobchuk Viacheslav/Shutterstock Images, 9 (top); Jarun Ontakrai/Shutterstock Images, 9 (bottom); kali9/iStockphoto, 11; xmee/Shutterstock Images, 13 (bottom), 16 (bottom right); kate_sept2004/iStockphoto, 15 (bottom); wavebreakmedia/Shutterstock Images, 16 (top left); K images/Shutterstock Images, 16 (top right); Arkadiusz Fajer/Shutterstock Images, 16 (bottom left)

Library of Congress Cataloging-in-Publication Data
Names: Stratton, Connor, author.
Title: We help at home / by Connor Stratton.
Description: Lake Elmo, MN : Focus Readers, [2020] | Series: Activities we do
  Audience: K to grade 3 | Includes index.
Identifiers: LCCN 2019006770 (print) | LCCN 2019009381 (ebook) | ISBN
  9781641859936 (pdf) | ISBN 9781641859363 (ebook) | ISBN 9781641857987
  (hardcover) | ISBN 9781641858670 (pbk.)
Subjects: LCSH: Home economics--Juvenile literature. | Housekeeping--Juvenile literature.
Classification: LCC TX148 (ebook) | LCC TX148 .S77 2020 (print) | DDC
  648--dc23
LC record available at https://lccn.loc.gov/2019006770

Printed in the United States of America
Mankato, MN
May, 2019

About the Author

Connor Stratton loves cooking at home, eating popcorn, and watching movies with friends. He lives in Minnesota.

Table of Contents

Helping Together 5

Making a Meal 8

Washing Sheets 12

Glossary 16

Index 16

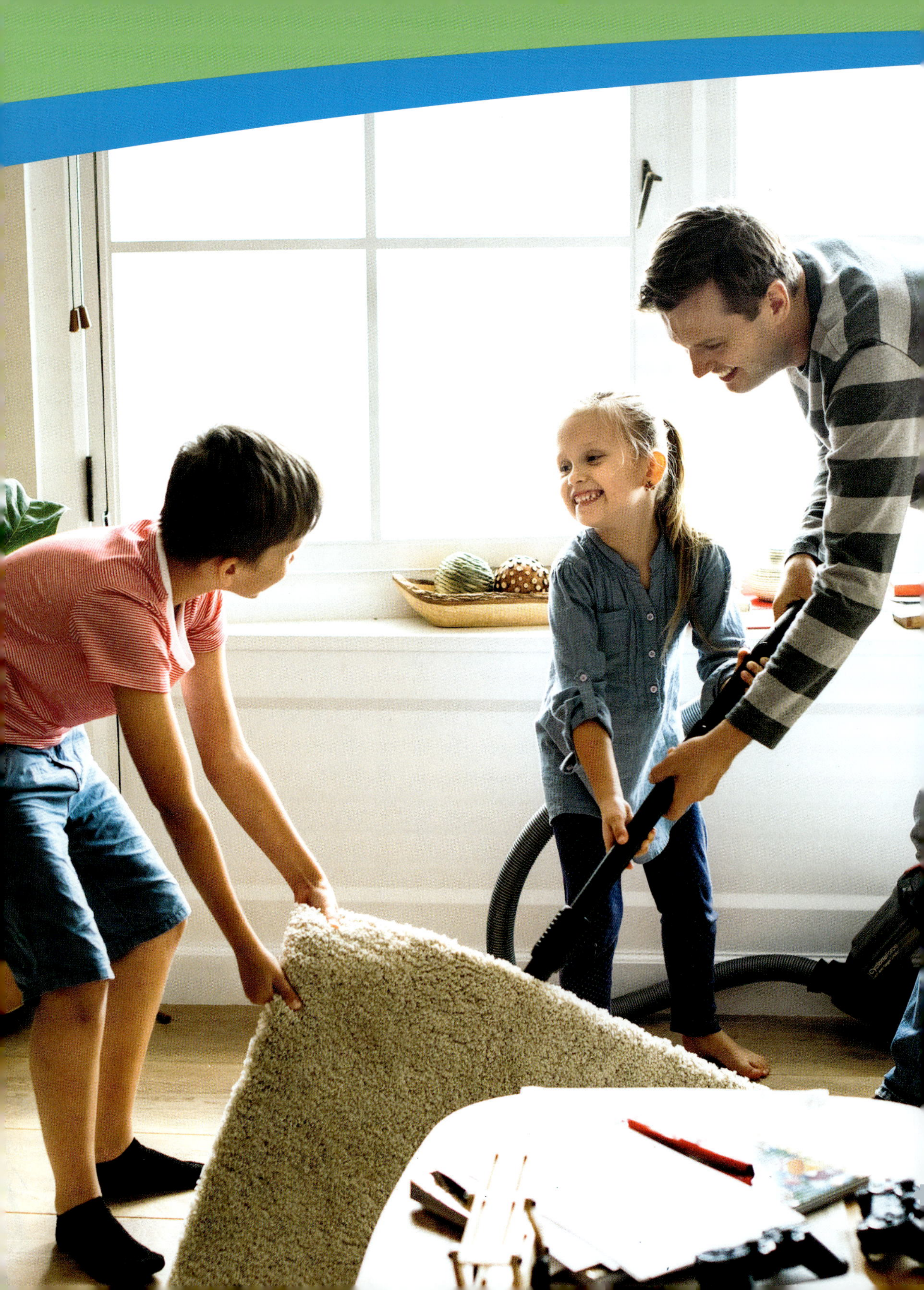

Helping Together

We help at home.

We all work together.

The floor needs to stay clean.

We sweep with a **broom**.

We clean the rug.

broom

floor

rug

7

Making a Meal

We help cook meals.

We help crack the **eggs**.

We help mix the eggs.

eggs

9

We help set the table.

We set the **forks**.

We set the knives.

We set the plates.

fork

knife

plate

11

Washing Sheets

We help wash the sheets.

We take sheets off the bed.

We put the sheets in the **washer**.

sheets

bed

washer

13

The sheets are clean.

We take out the sheets.

We help make the bed.

15

Glossary

broom

forks

eggs

washer

Index

E
eggs, 8

F
floor, 6

S
sheets, 12, 14

T
table, 10